The Joyful Colourist™

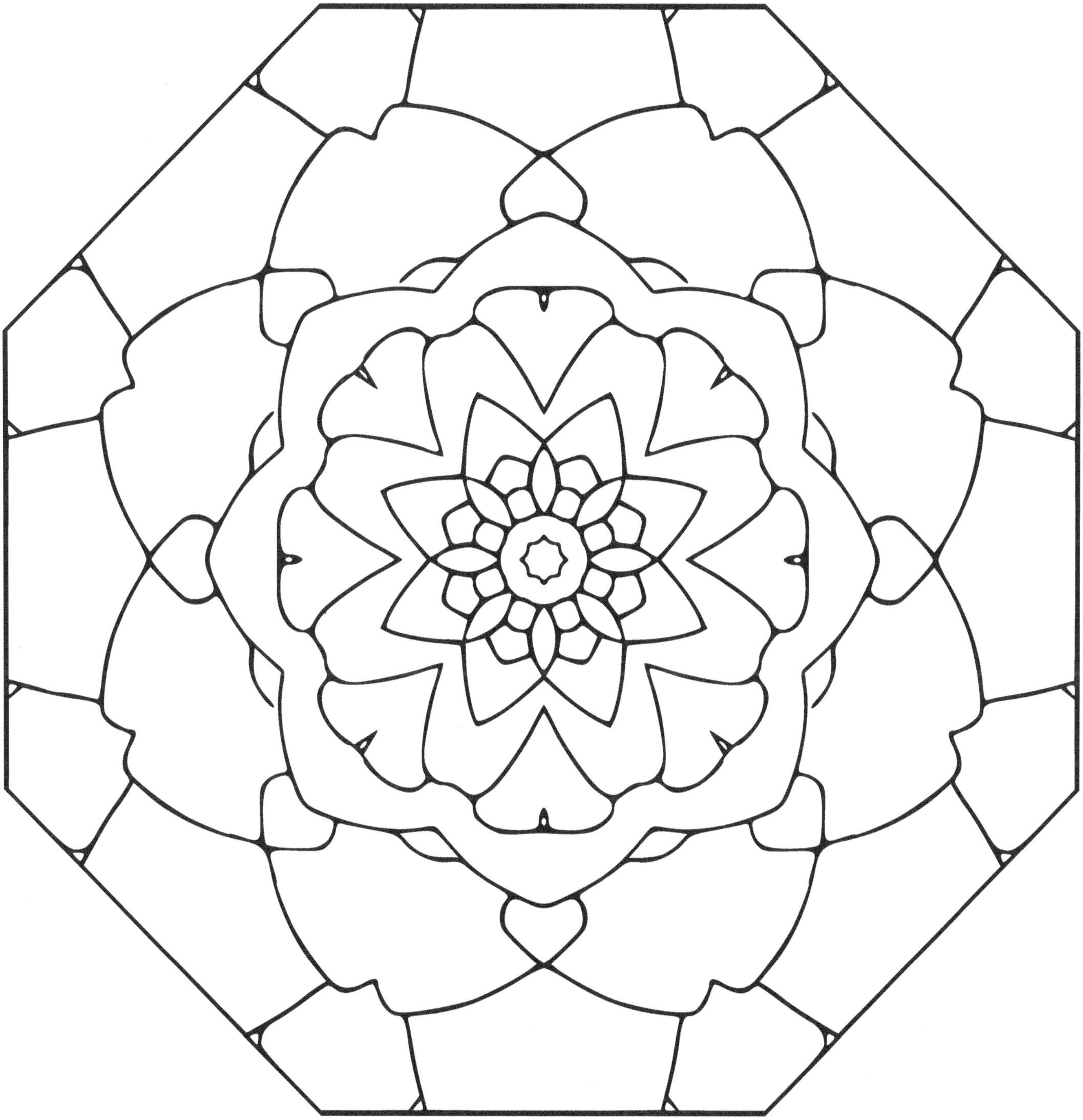

Explore Mandalas (Volume 4)

The Joyful Colourist™

Explore Mandalas (Volume 4)

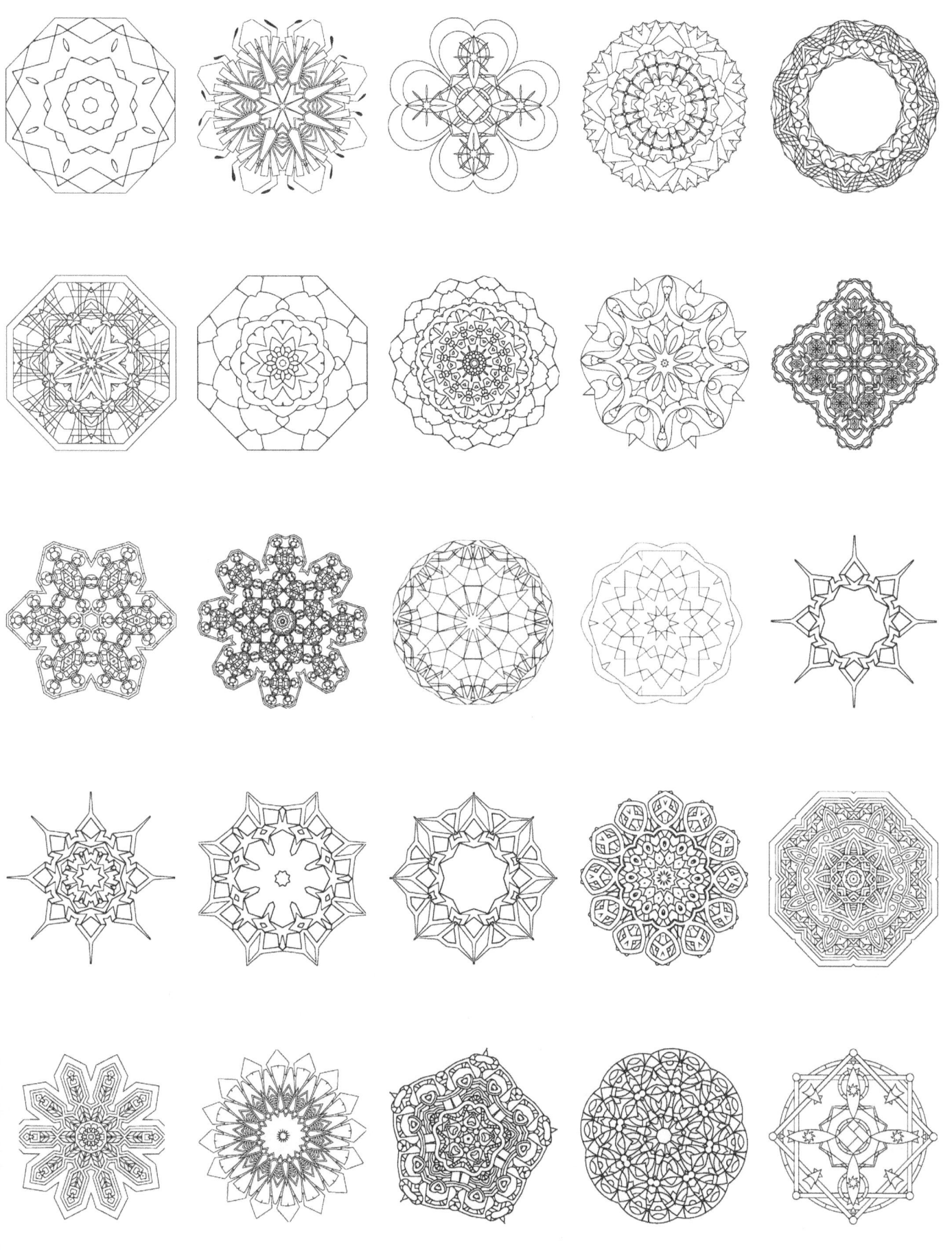

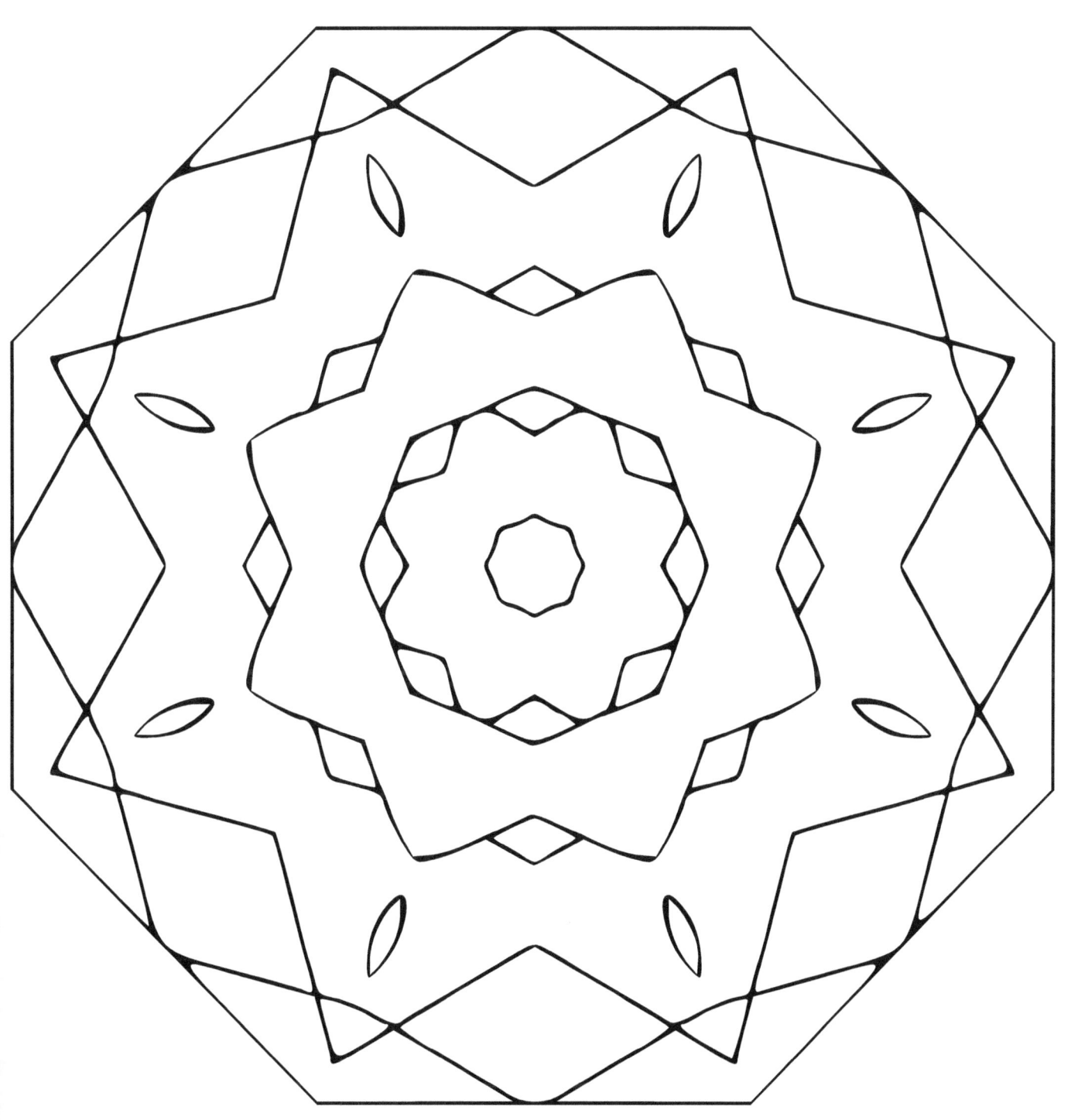

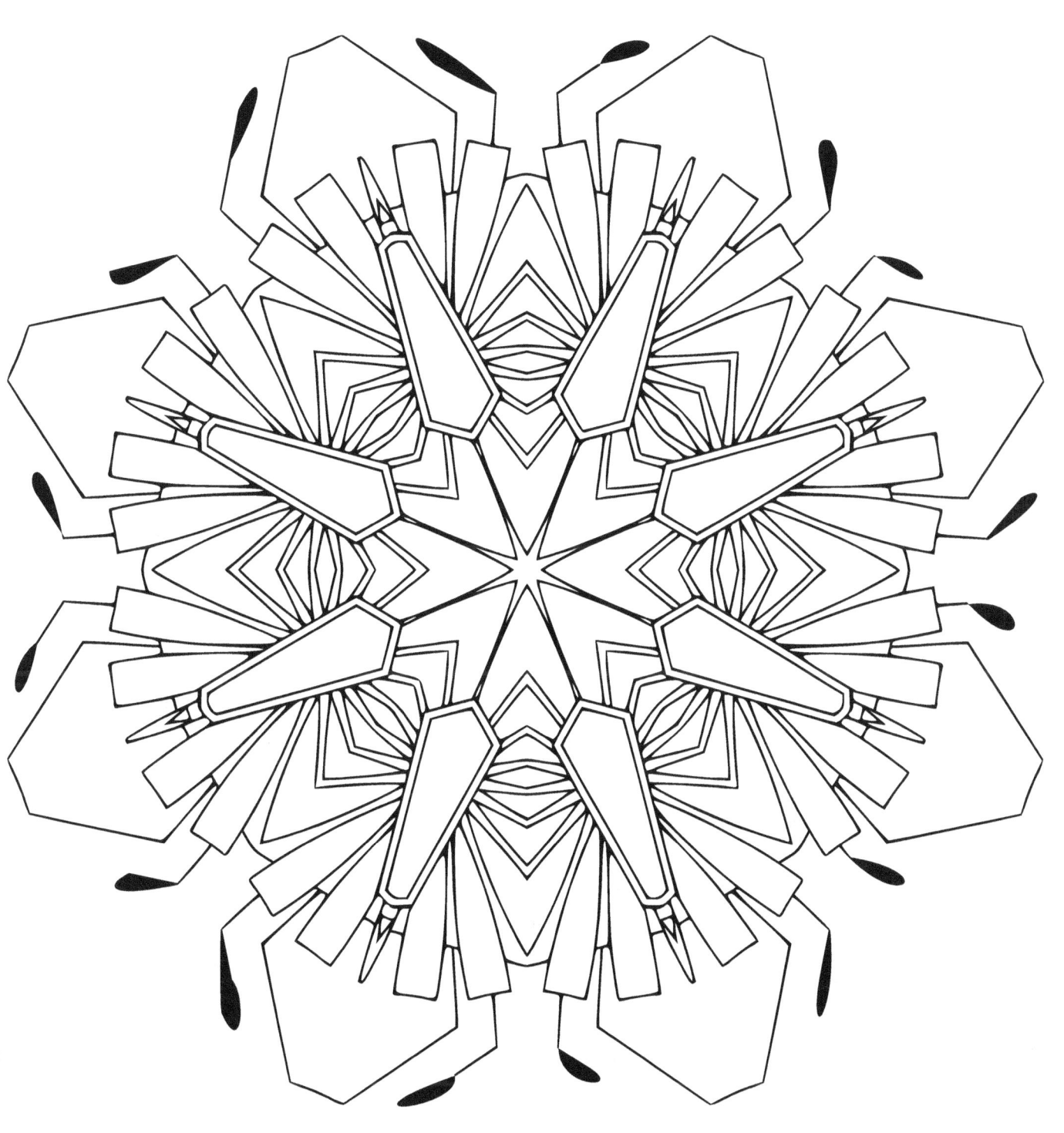

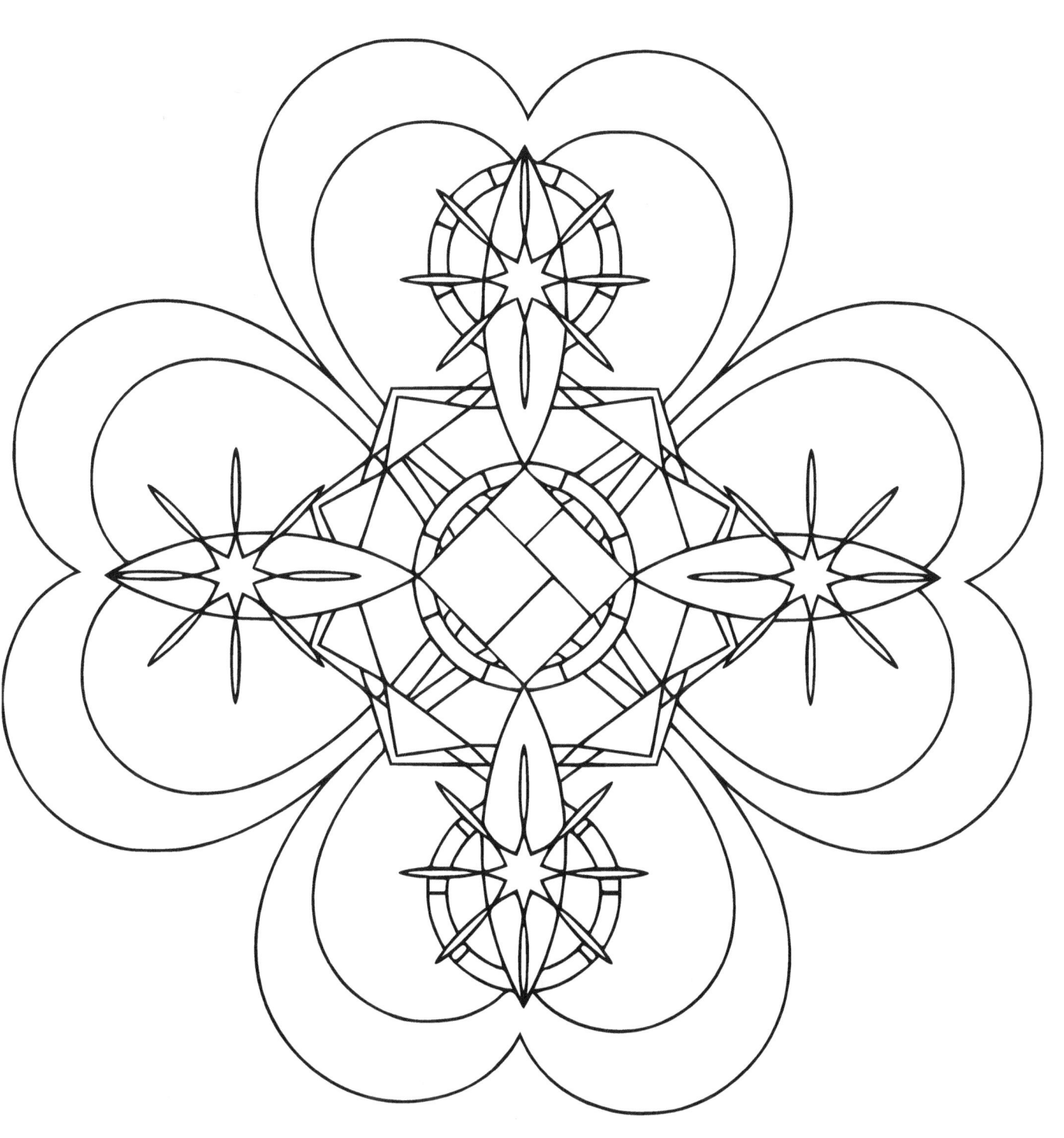

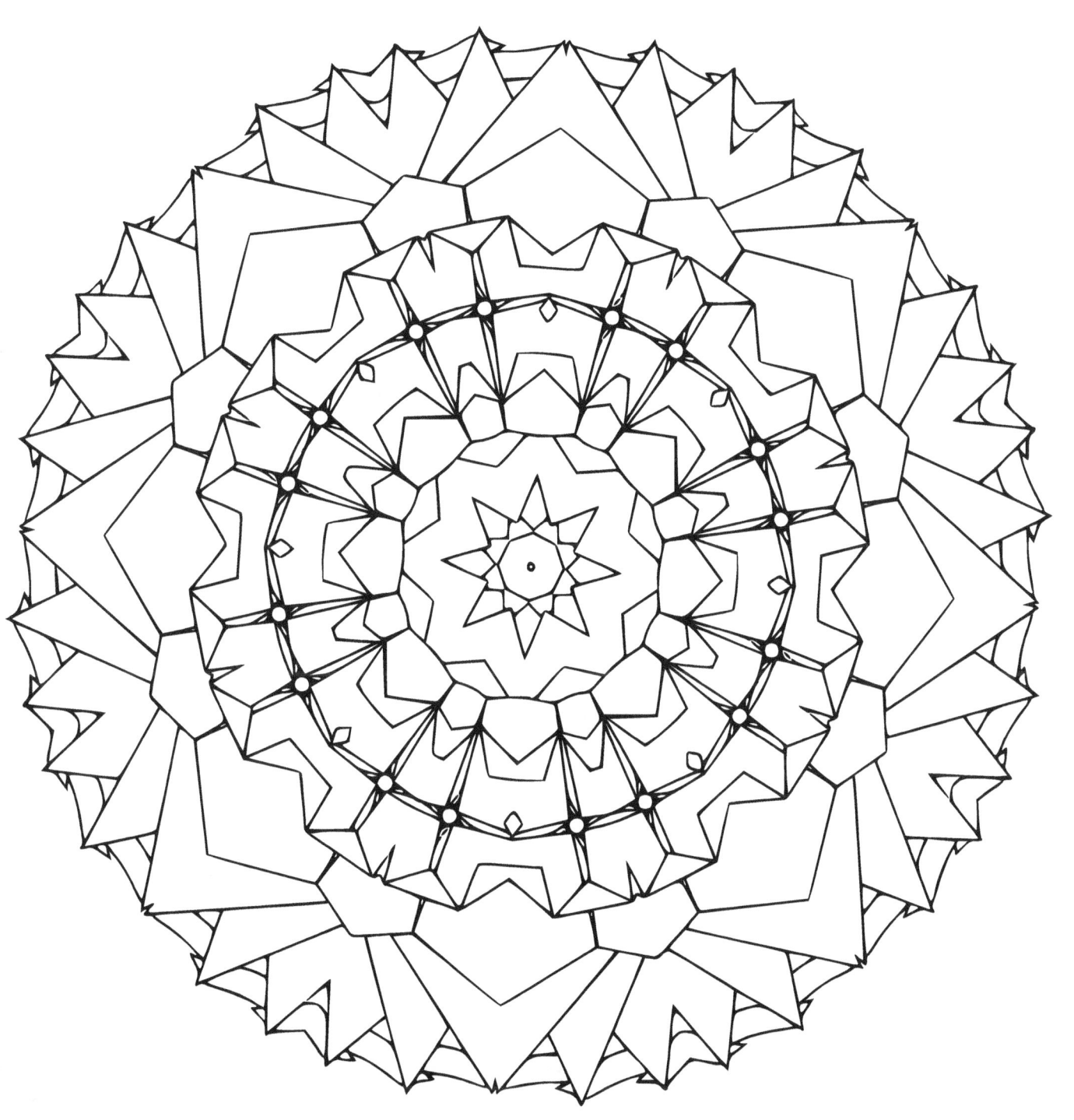

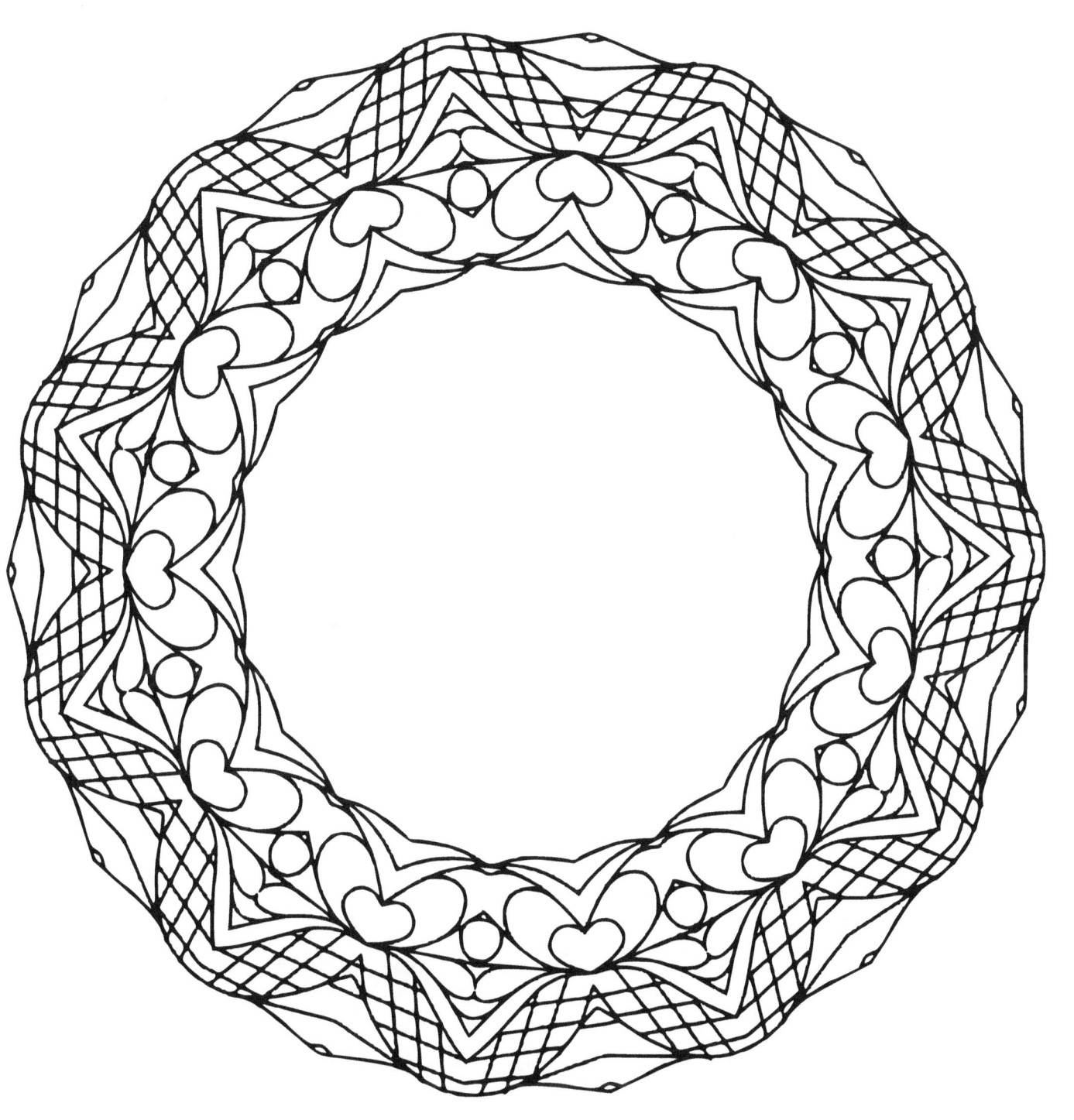

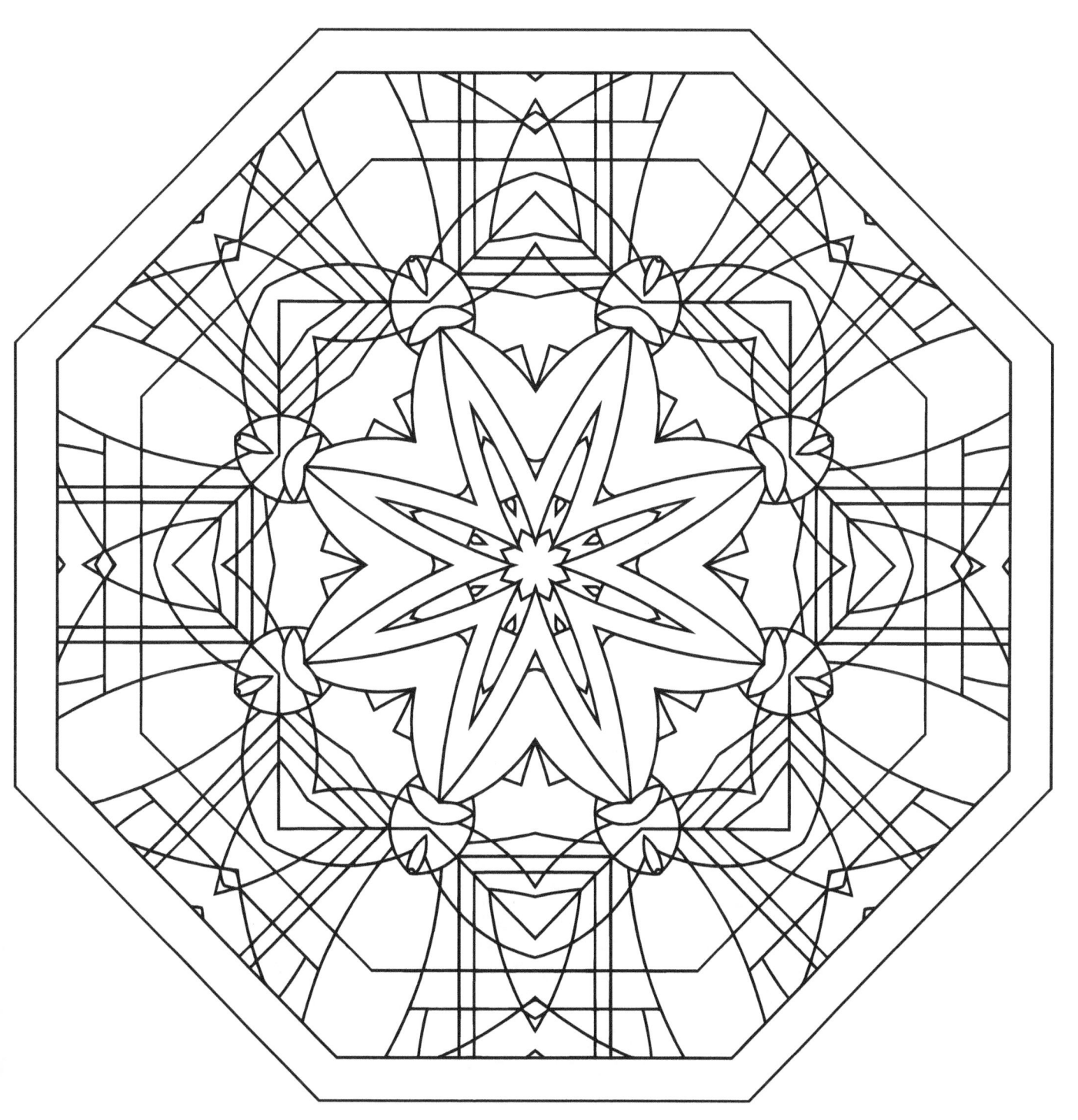

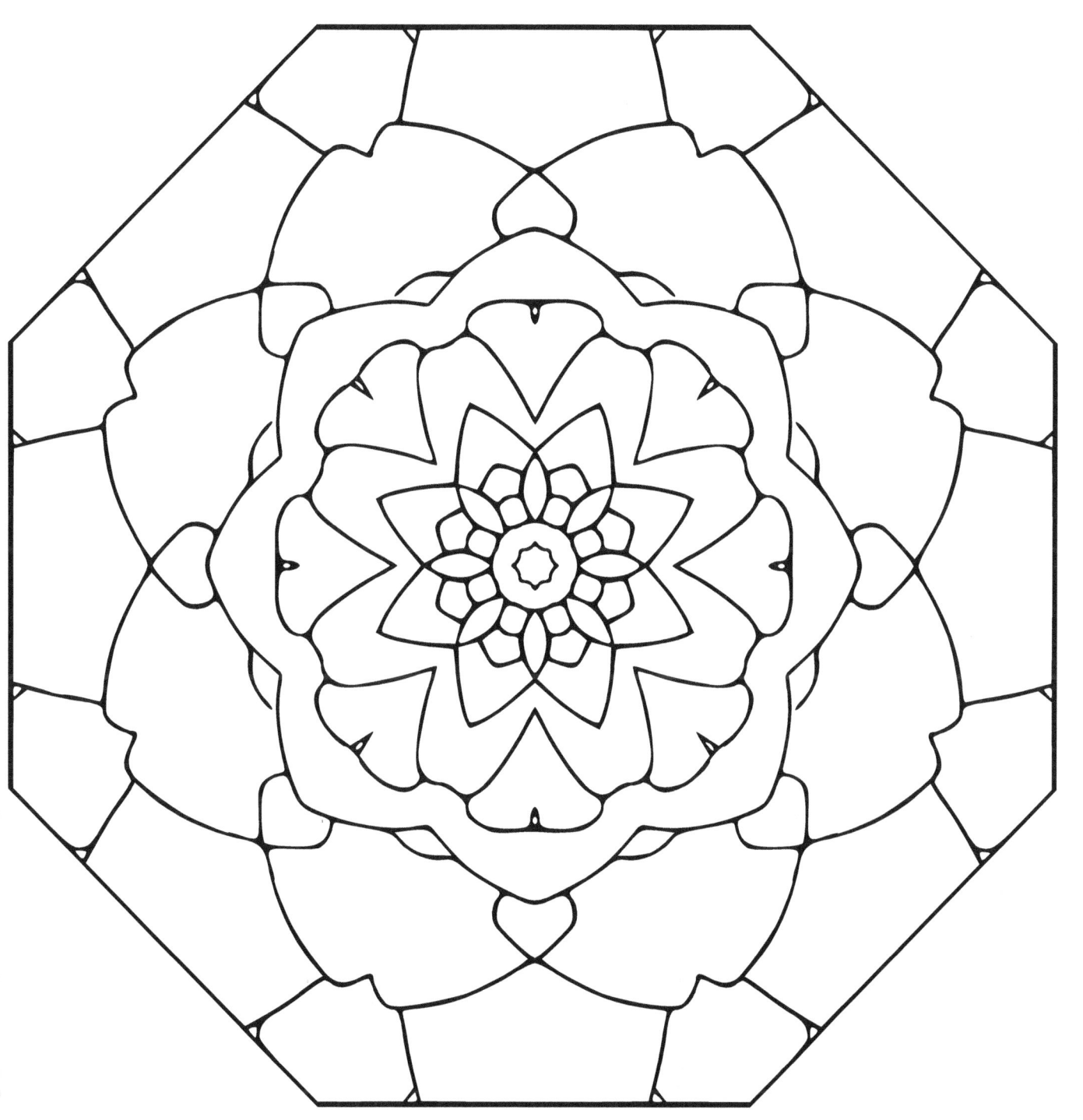

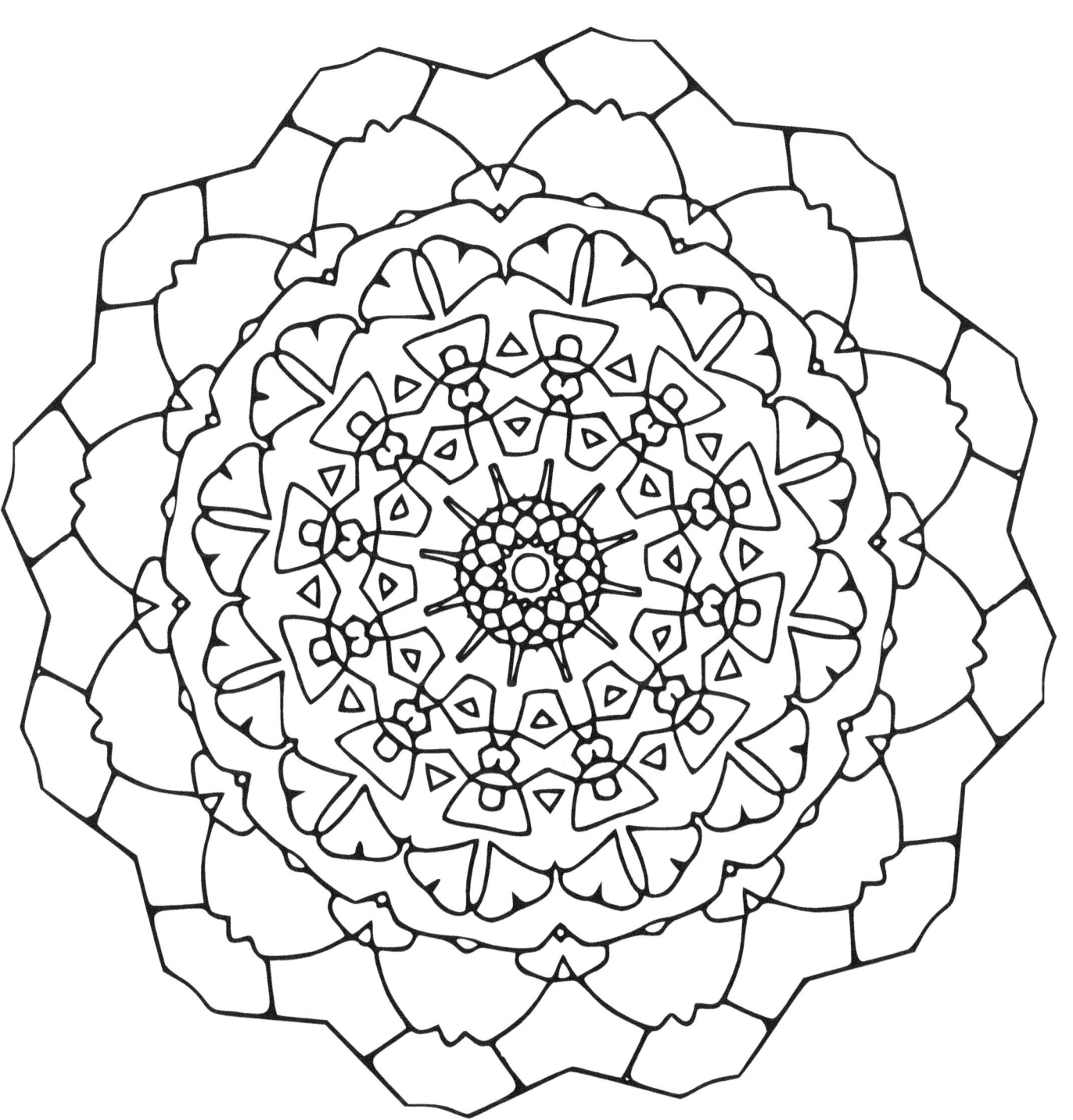

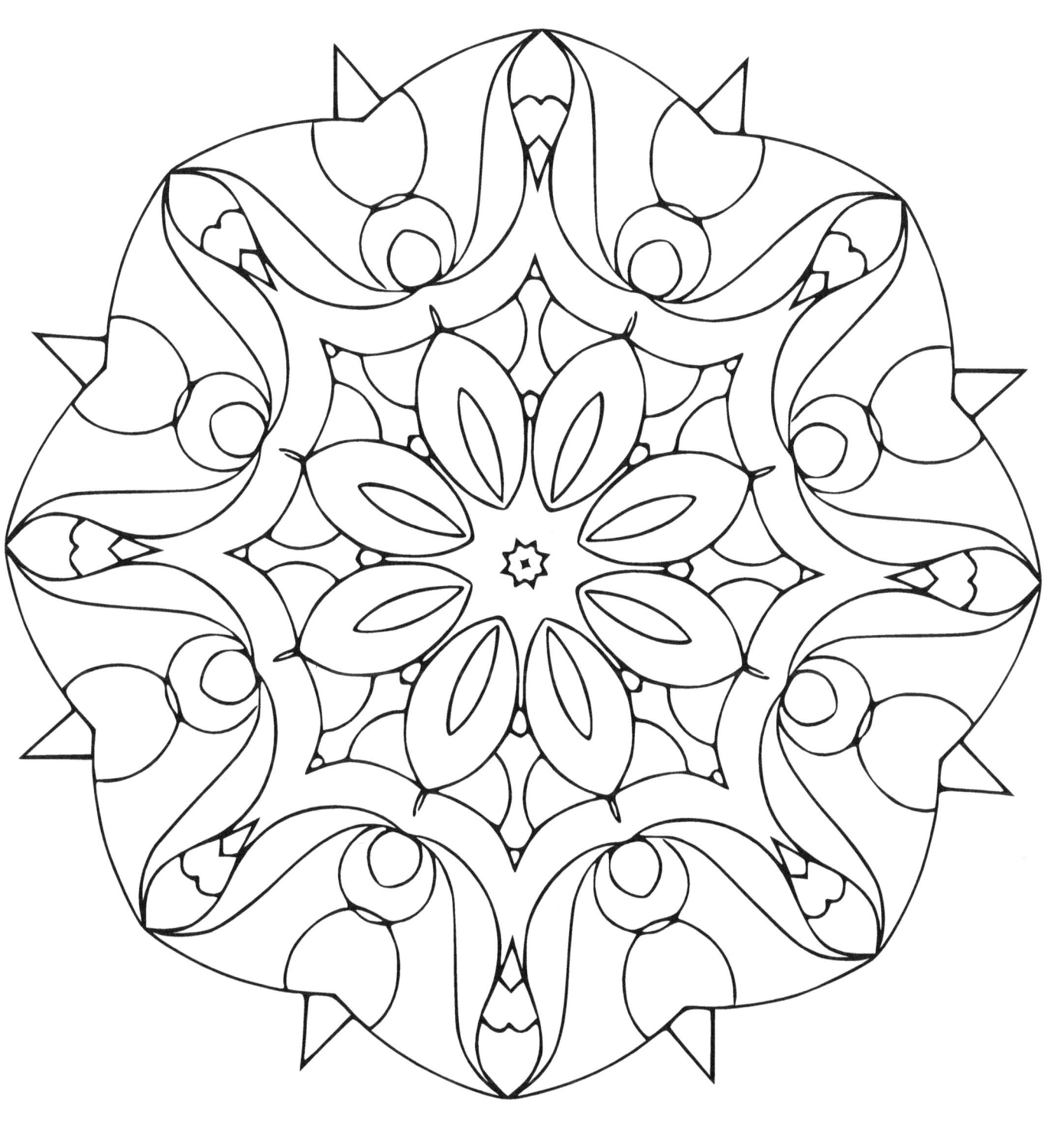

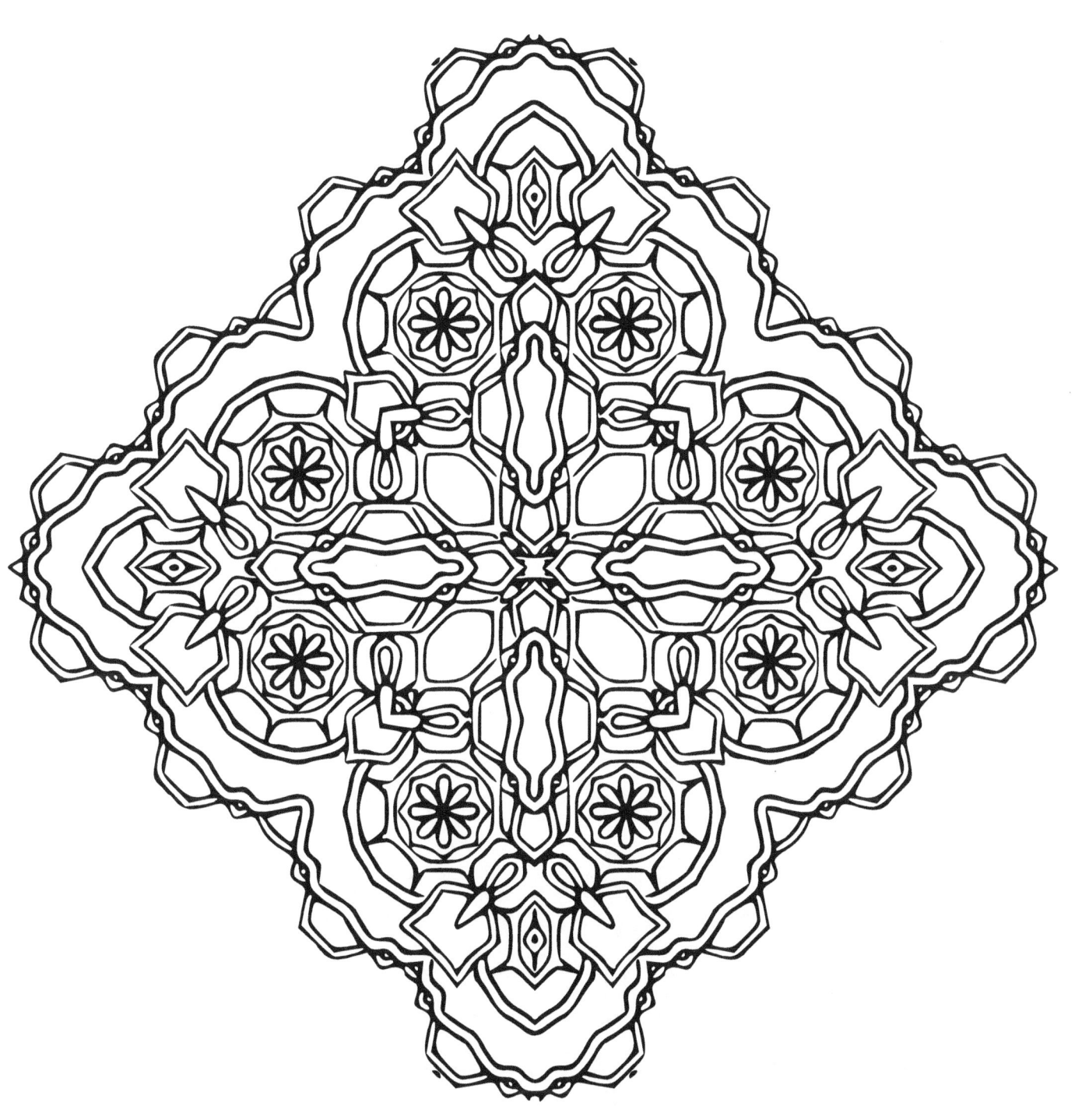

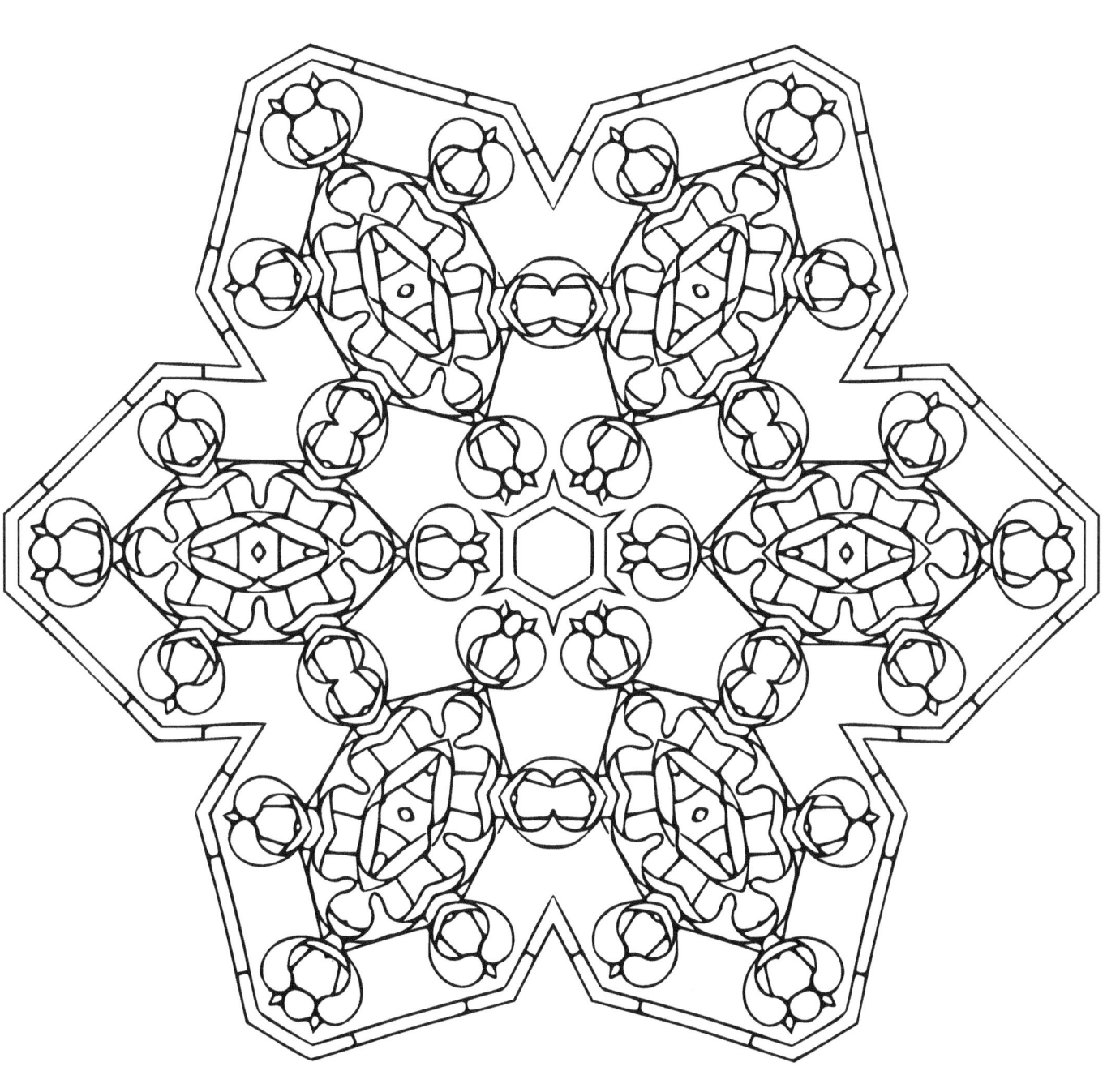

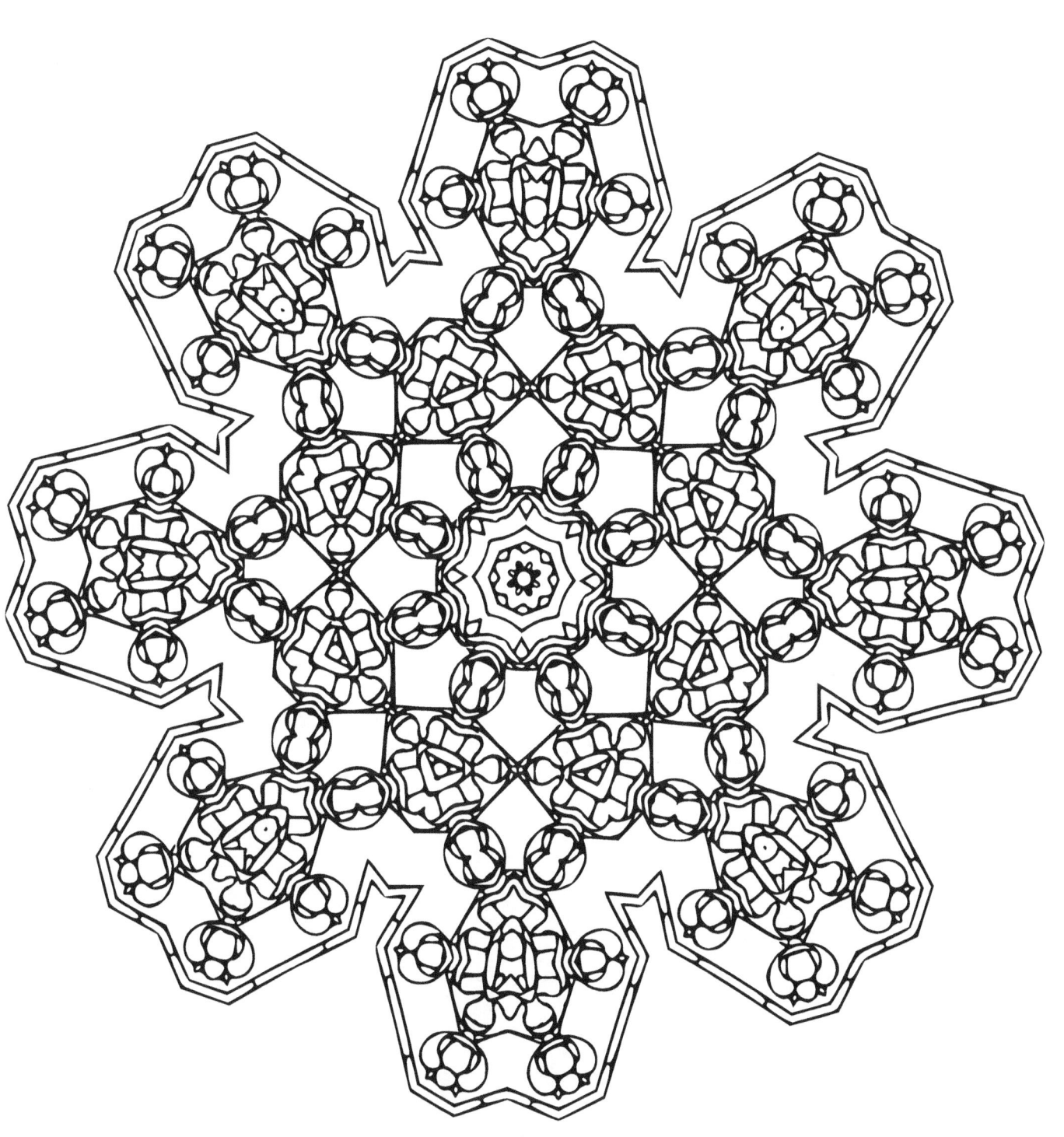

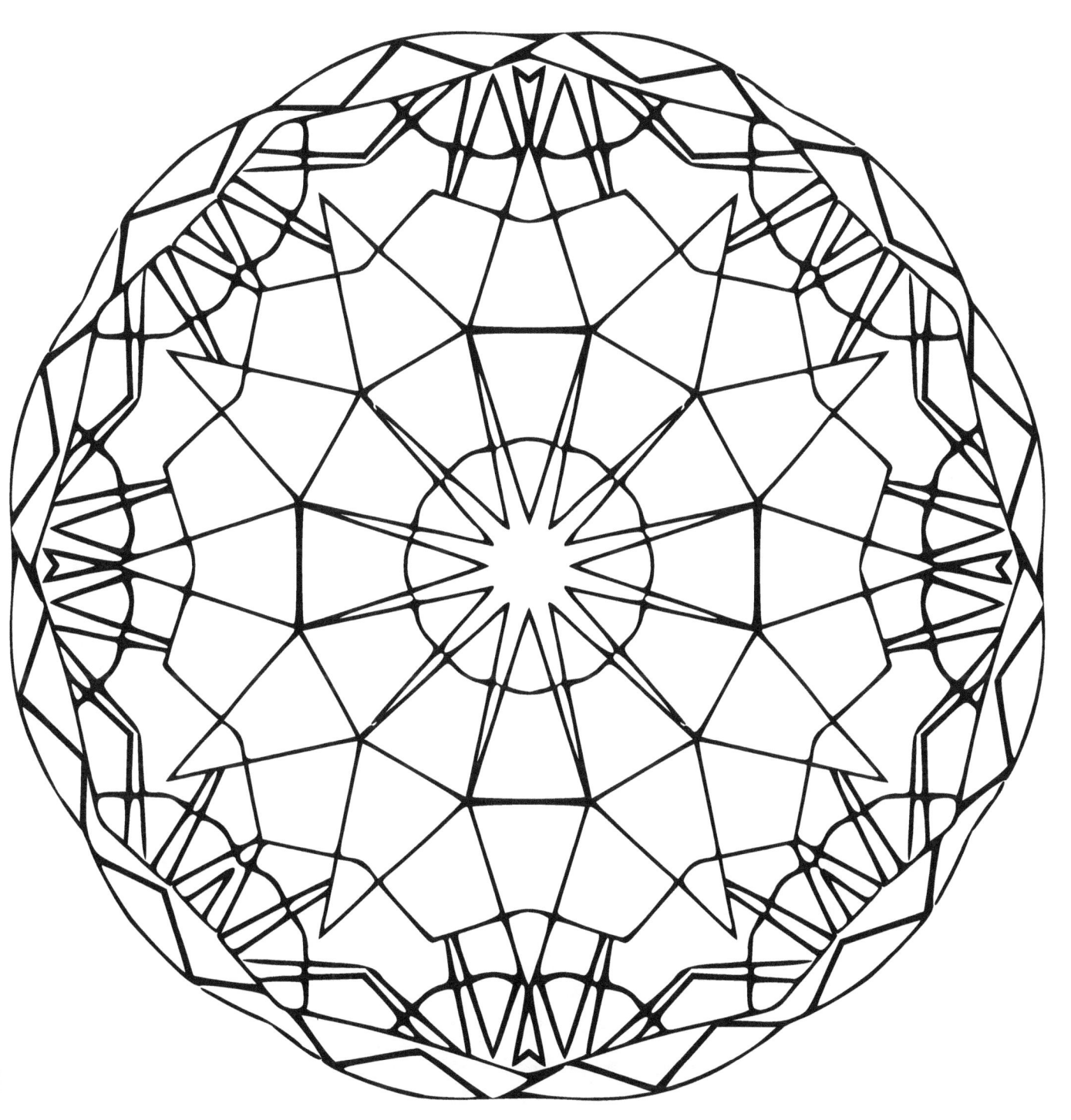

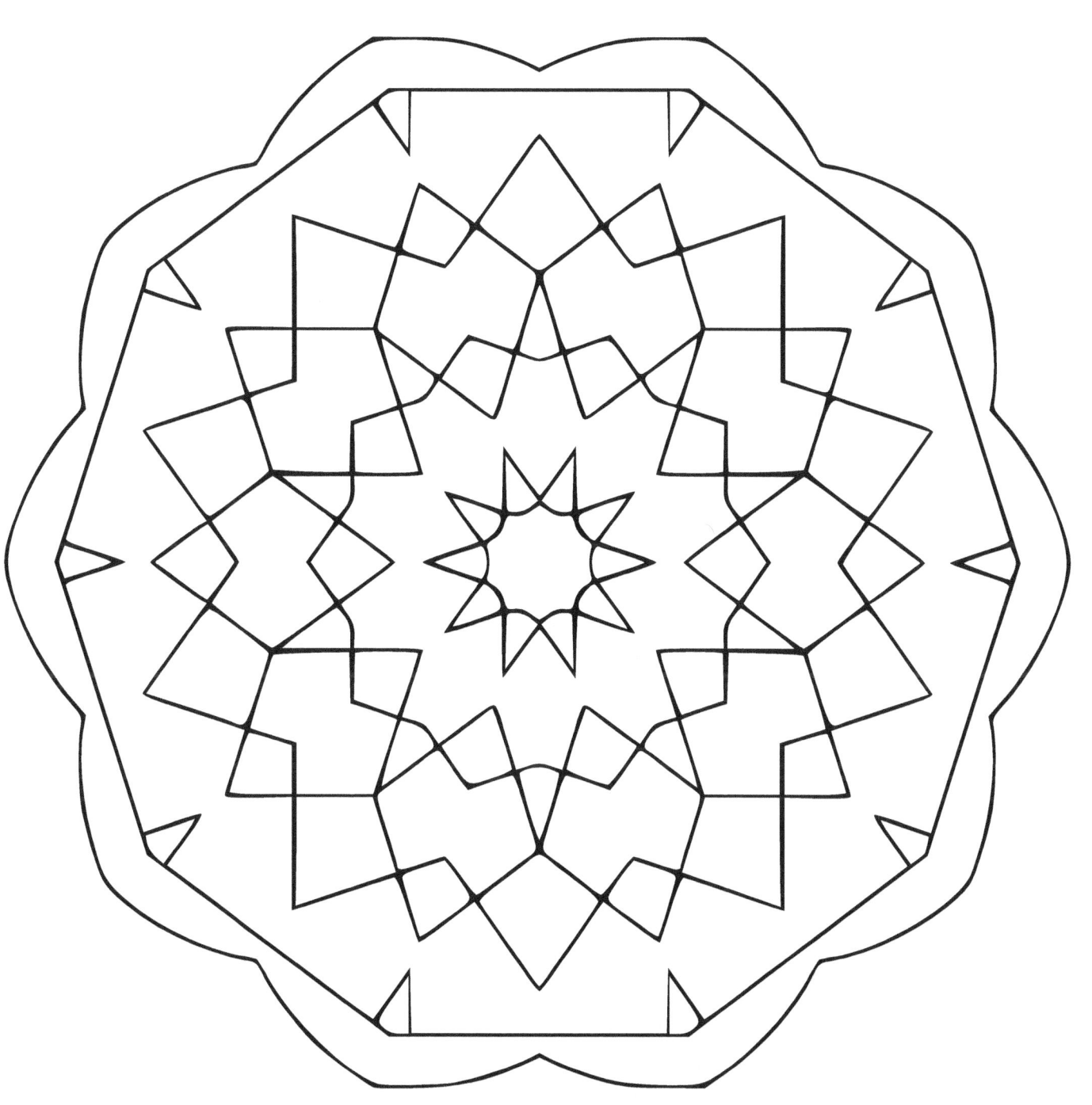

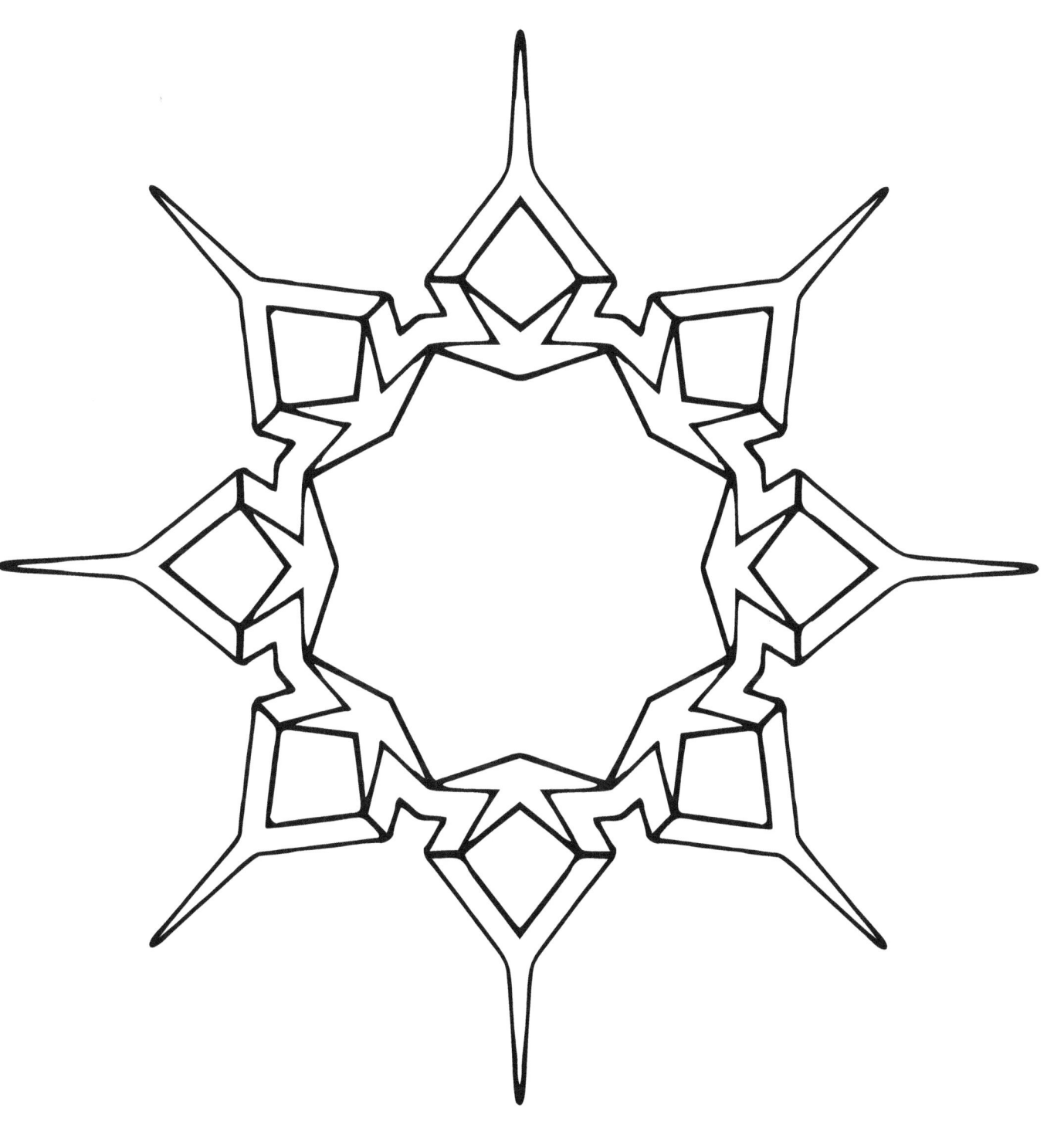

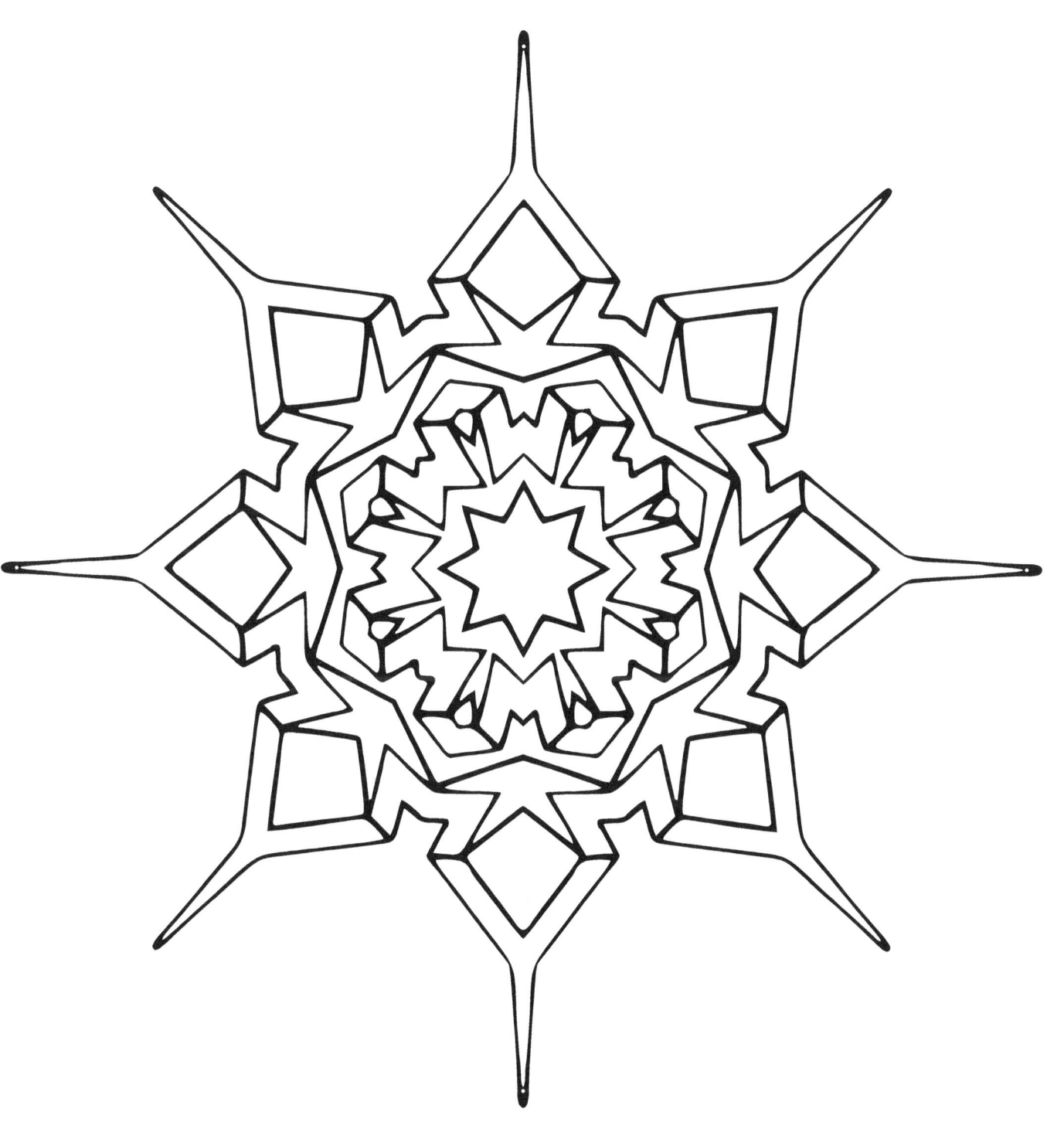

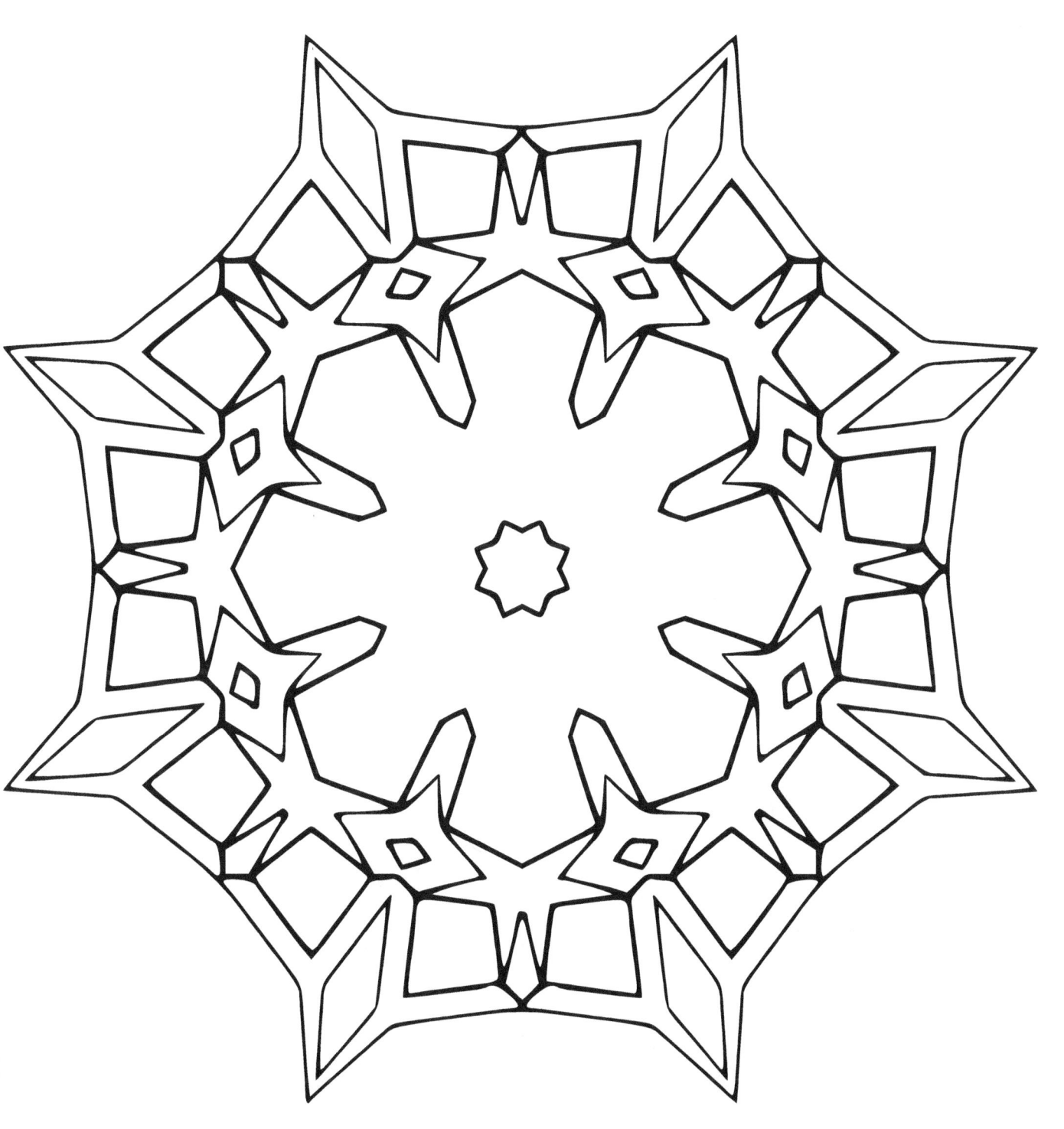

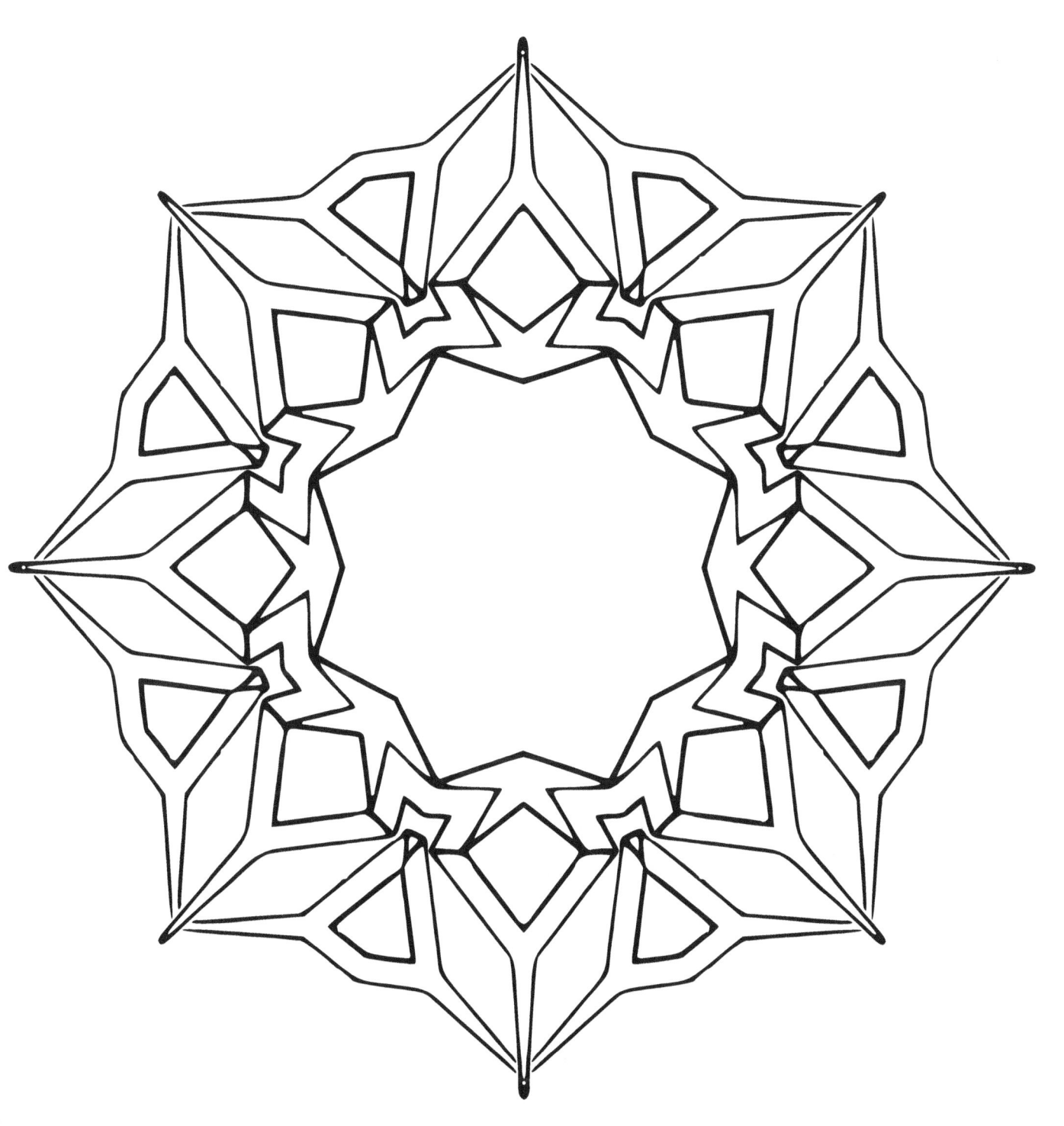

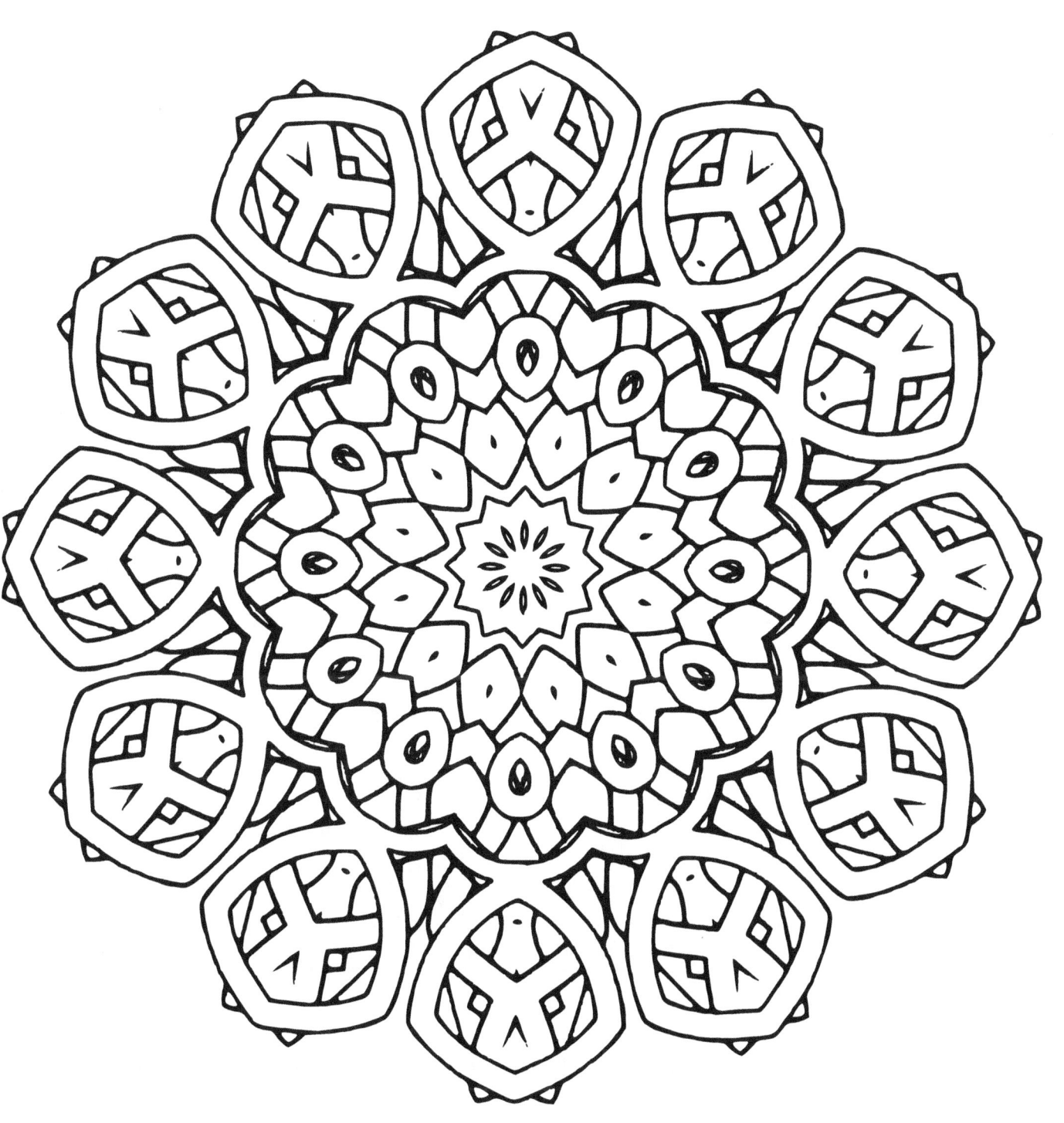

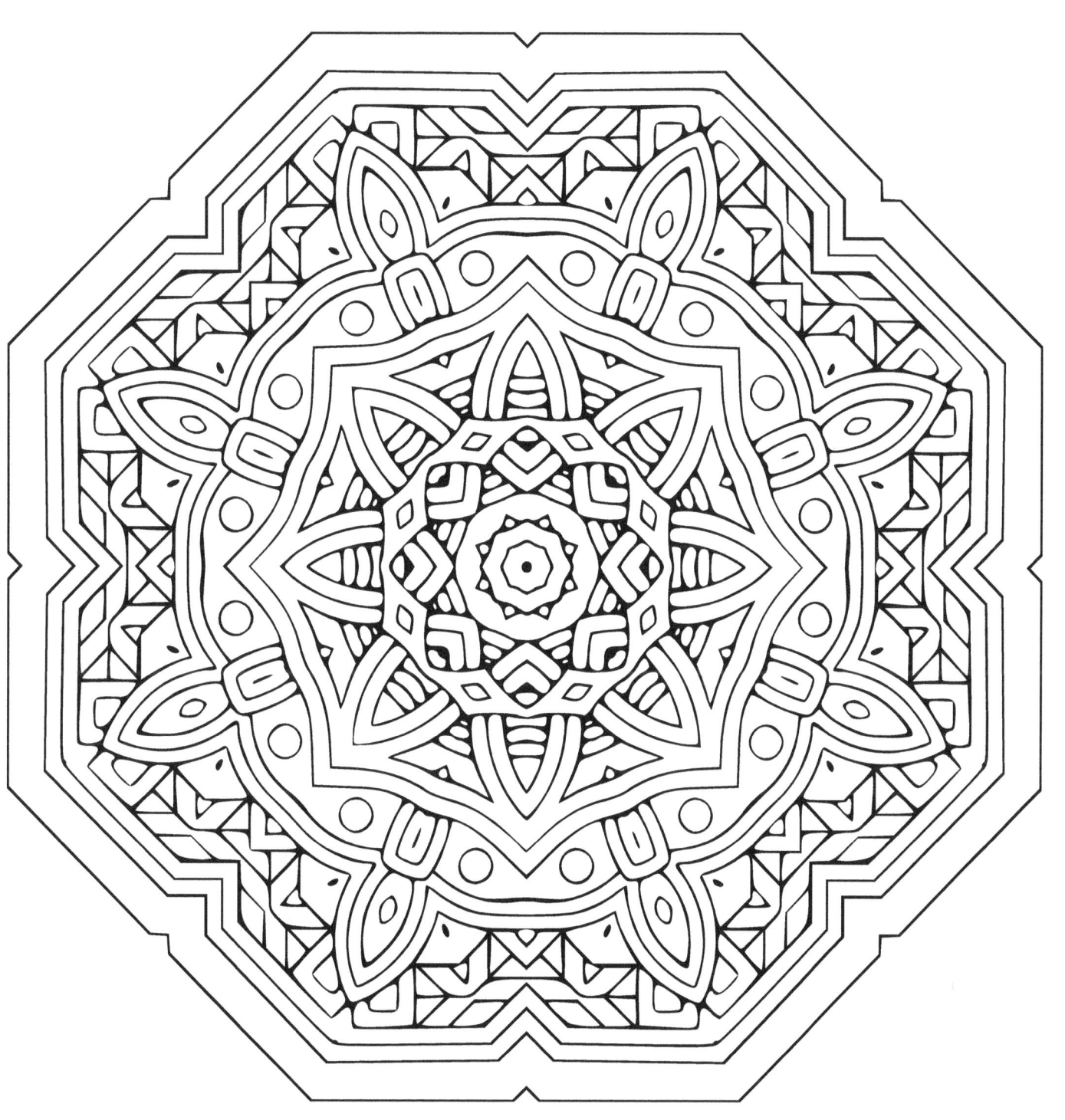

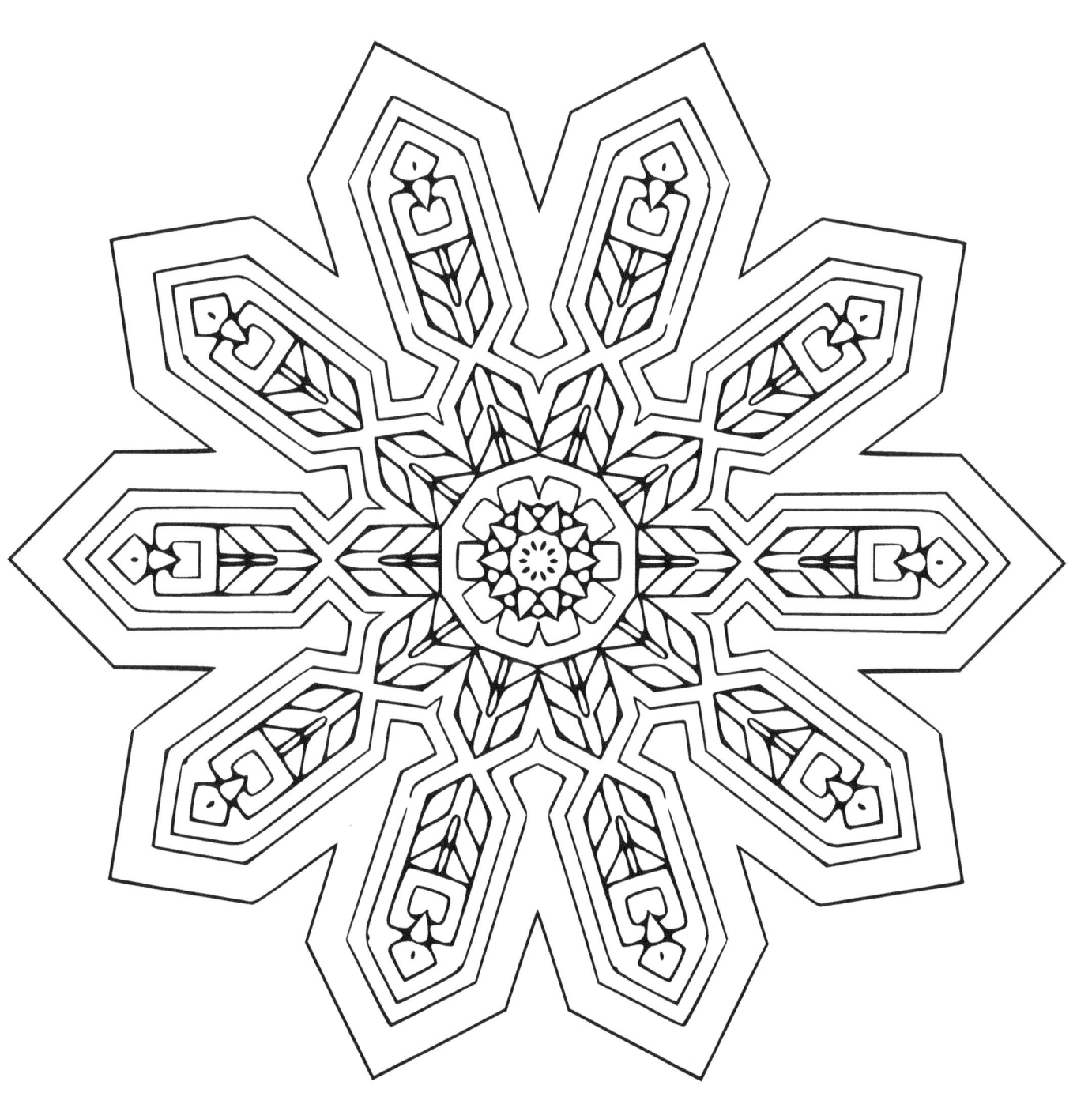

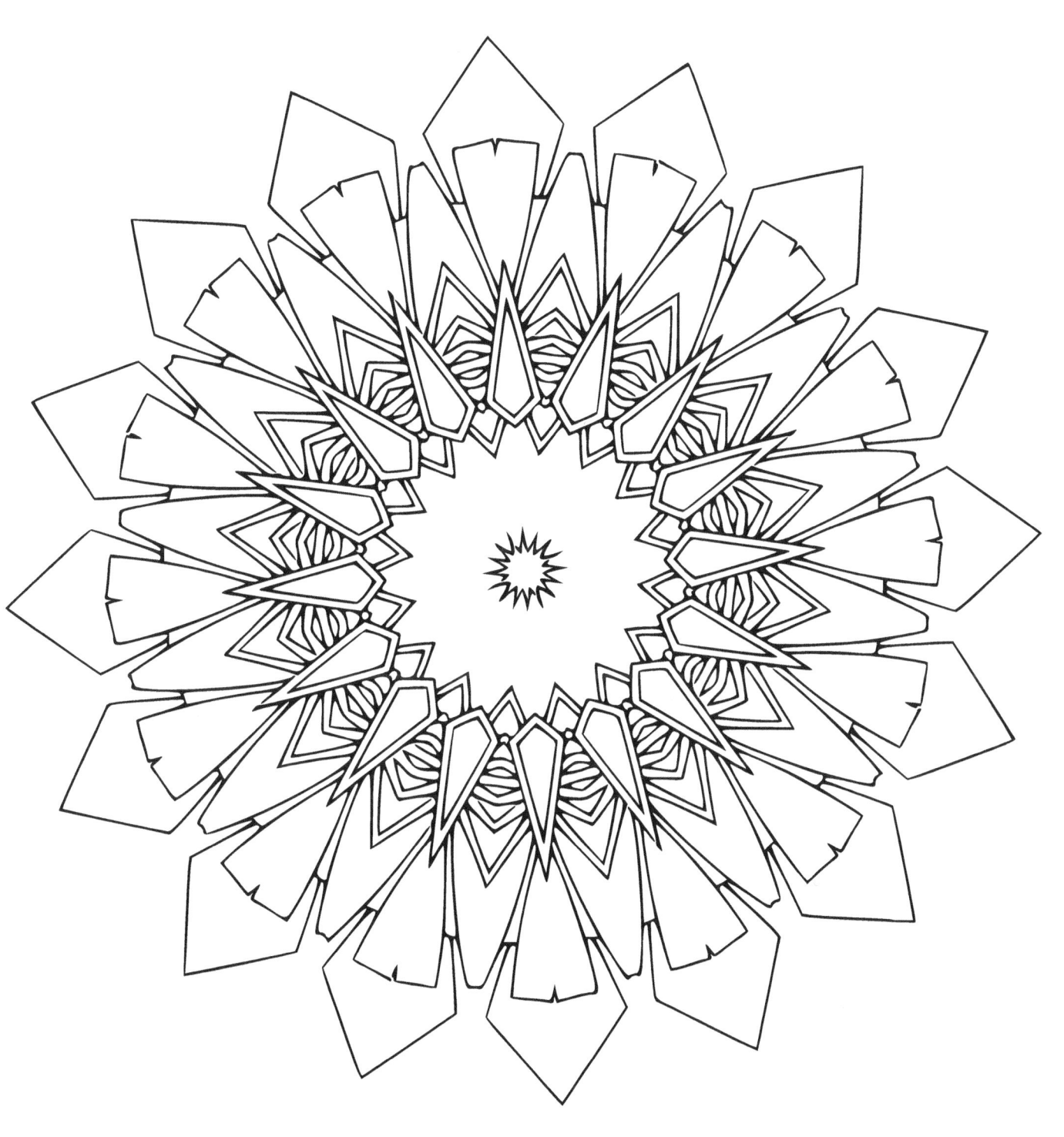

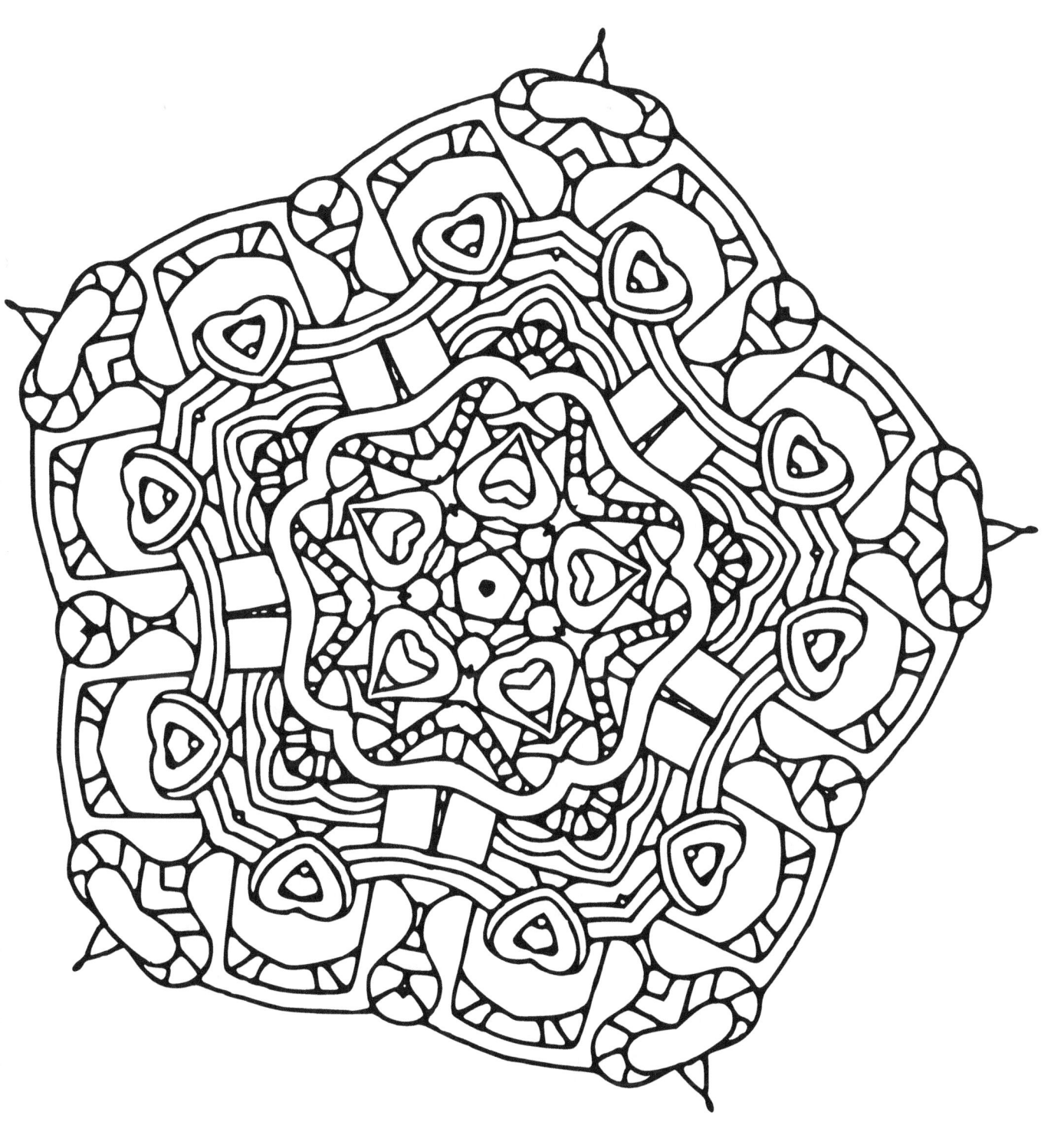

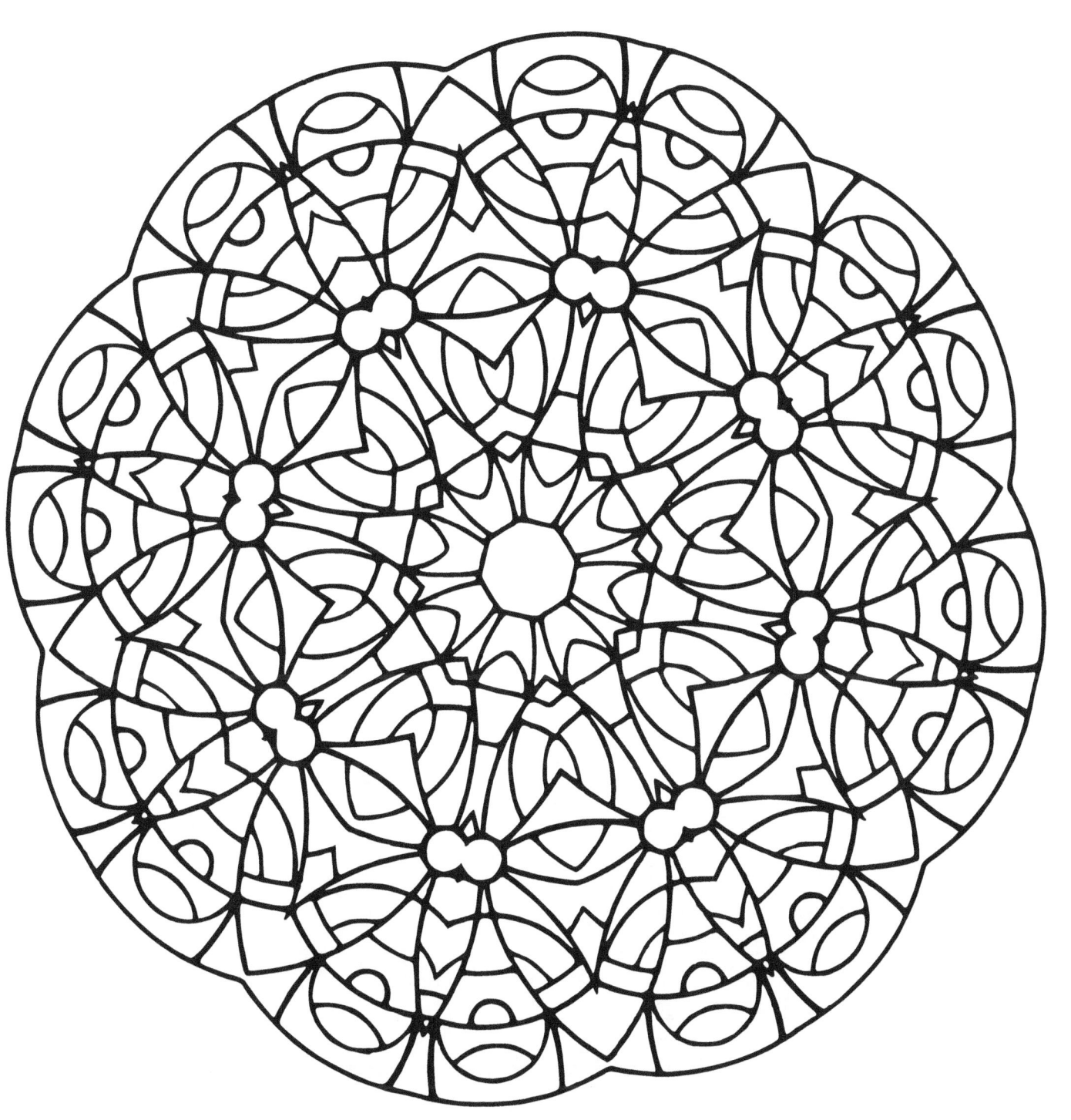

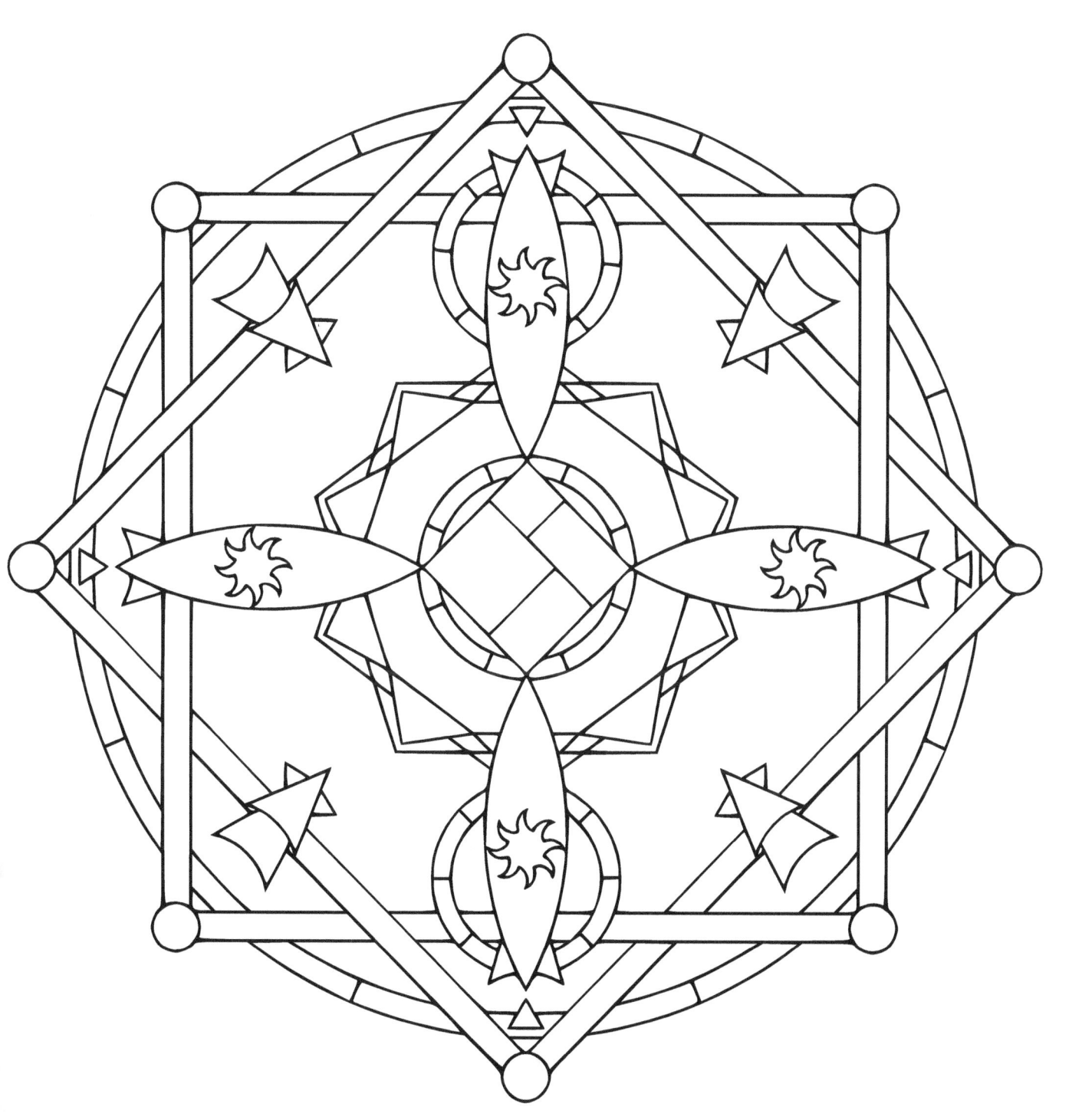

The Joyful Colourist™ Explore Mandalas Series

http://joyfulcolourist.com

The Joyful Colourist™

Explore Mandalas (Volume 1)

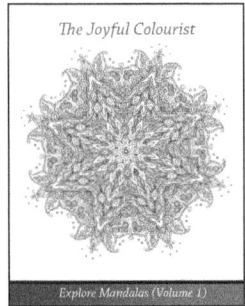

The Joyful Colourist™

Explore Mandalas (Volume 2)

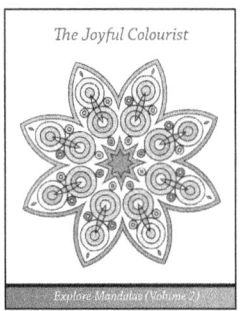

The Joyful Colourist™

Explore Mandalas (Volume 3)

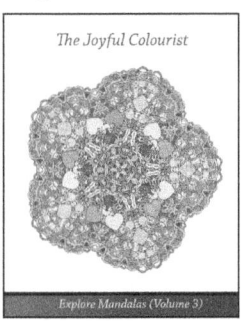

The Joyful Colourist™

Explore Mandalas (Volume 4)

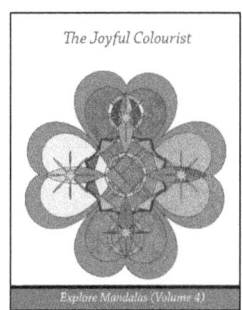

The Joyful Colourist™

Explore Mandalas (Volume 5)

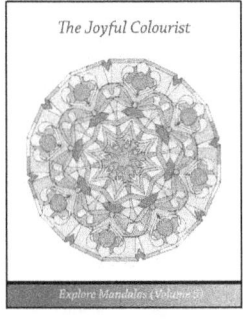

The Joyful Colourist™

Explore Mandalas (Volume 6)

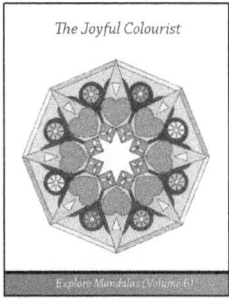